LOOK!

Zoom in on Art!

LOOK!

Zoom in on Art!

Gillian Wolfe

F

FRANCES LINCOLN
CHILDREN'S BOOKS

PHOTOGRAPHIC ACKNOWLEDGMENTS

For permission to reproduce the paintings on the following pages and for supplying
photographs, the Publishers would like to thank:

AKG, London/Erich Lessing: front cover, 2-3 & 20-21, 24
Bridgeman Art Library: 10-11 (© Estate of Eric Ravilious 2002. All rights reserved, DACS),
12-13, 22-23 (© DACS 2002), 25, 26-27, 30-31(© 2002 Bridget Riley. All rights reserved.
Courtesy Karsten Schubert, London)
Dulwich Picture Gallery, London: back cover, 1, 16, 28-29
Hirschl & Adler Galleries, New York: 7
Mauritshuis, The Hague: 14-15
Photo © 1977 The Metropolitan Museum of Art: 8 (courtesy of the Estate of
Georges Schreiber and the Susan Teller Gallery, New York)
Photo © 2002 The Museum of Modern Art, New York: 9 (© 2002 Mondrian/Holtzman
Trust c/o Beeldrecht, Amsterdam, Holland & DACS, London)
The National Gallery, London: 17
The Royal Collection © 2002, Her Majesty Queen Elizabeth II: 18-19
© Angela Thomas Schmid/prolitteris: 32-33
(© ADAGP, Paris and DACS, London 2002)
Collection of Whitney Museum of American Art, New York: 6

LOOK! Zoom in on Art! © Frances Lincoln Limited 2002
Text copyright © Gillian Wolfe 2002

First published in the UK by Frances Lincoln Children's Books
and in the USA by Oxford University Press in 2002.

This edition published in the USA in 2007 by
Frances Lincoln Children's Books, 4 Torriano Mews,
Torriano Avenue, London NW5 2RZ
www.franceslincoln.com

British Library Cataloguing in Publication Data available on request

ISBN 978-1-84507-796-9

Printed in Singapore

1 3 5 7 9 8 6 4 2

Contents

Look Up 6

Look Down 8

Look Outside 10

Look Inside..................... 12

Look Through................. 14

Look Behind 16

Look Close Up 18

Look All Around 20

Look Quickly.................. 22

Look Again 24

Look and Stare............... 26

Look, but Peep 28

Look If You Can.............. 30

Look Inwards................. 32

Look It Up.....................34

Index 40

Look Up

A daring and terrifying moment is captured in paint. Looking **up** we see a trapeze artist swinging forward to catch his acrobat partner, who is performing a triple somersault through space. It looks brilliantly effortless, but is actually very dangerous and takes years of practice; they cannot make a mistake.

This artist lived with circus people for three months to sketch their exciting, daredevil performances.

The Flying Codonas – **John Steuart Curry**

You are looking *up* in the tent, yet you seem to be looking *down* at the top figure. Why?

Turn the picture upside down. Can you describe how the figures now look completely different?

Your gaze seems to race **up** the vertical sides of the jostling skyscrapers to the tiny patches of blue sky at the top. The buildings look real enough – yet they are quite different from a photograph. In what way?

Turn the picture upside down; now do you feel that you are looking up or down?

Try this: sit at a table and draw any object you like that is level with your eye. Then sit on the floor, look up and draw it again. Lay the drawings side by side and compare the results.

Windows – **Charles Sheeler**

Look Down

Looking **down** into the circus ring from the top of the tent, you see the lively ringmaster in charge of romping white horses, leaping clowns and acrobatic bareback riders.

To amuse his young daughter Joan, this artist wrote a book about the adventures of Bambino the Clown. He illustrated it with water-colour pictures like this one.

How has the artist given the impression that the animals and people are moving at frantic speed?

Do you think these clowns are clumsy, or are they really very skilled?

Three Clowns in a Ring – **Georges Schreiber**

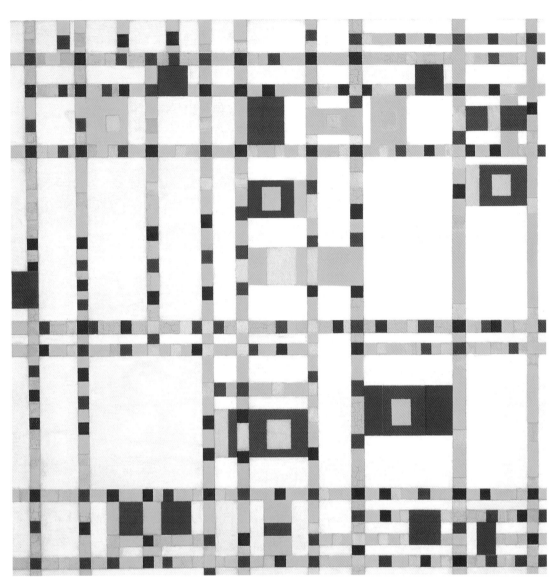

Broadway Boogie Woogie –
Piet Mondrian

Imagine that you are looking out of a top floor window of one of the towering buildings on page 7. As you gaze **down** from that tremendous height you see the straight, grid-like American city streets far below. Tiny shapes – people and traffic – seem to buzz between the skyscrapers, almost as if the city is dancing to jazzy 'boogie woogie' music.

Try a 'birds eye view' drawing. Perhaps look down from your window, or go outside and sketch creatures scuttling through the undergrowth. You could even look down and draw your own feet!

Train Landscape – Eric Ravilious

Look Outside

The artist invites you to be a passenger gazing **out** of the window of a railway carriage.

You speed through the countryside and suddenly see a spectacular white horse carved in the hillside. It may look tiny, but if you compare it with the size of the hills you realise how large it really is.

This is a third-class compartment in a steam train. Can you imagine what it was like to ride on a train like this? It had no corridor, no buffet car and no toilets, but it did have a puffing, clanking rhythm and a steamy hiss and wheeze that many people enjoyed.

The horse is one of a number of chalk figures carved into the landscape; some were made by ancient people who scraped away the thin turf to make shapes that could be seen for miles around. This horse is more recent – only about 200 years old.

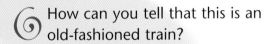 How can you tell that this is an old-fashioned train?

Are the white patches on the grass frost, snow, chalk or mist?

We often take a photograph to remember a certain place. Drawings are another way of recording places we have visited. Why not get into the habit of taking a sketchpad on every outing? You will build up memories and skill at the same time.

Look Inside

No one seems to mind a horse joining in the family meal. Outstretched hands offer tasty morsels to the cheeky intruder. Can you spot the patient dog awaiting his turn?

This picture was painted over a hundred years ago. The man hanging up the horse's harness is the innkeeper and his wife is feeding the horse. Their two children sit near the window; opposite is the grandmother (cutting bread) and a very young boy, who is the son of the artist. He must have enjoyed being part of the scene his father was painting.

Notice how the girl's attention is all on the horse while her brother doesn't bother to look up. He's more interested in tucking in to his meal.

One of the Family – Frederick George Cotman

Look at the way the grandmother cuts bread. How do you do it in your family?

How can you tell that this is a country family?

Do you think the pie looks delicious? The artist was afraid that it would spoil before the picture was finished. His wife had the idea of stuffing the inside with coal so that the pastry would hold its shape for days!

Look Through

All kinds of birds flutter, splash, peck and perch in this busy scene; you can almost hear the clucking, cooing, cheeping and ruffle of wings.

Let your eye wander through the picture. Start with the young girl who has laid her hat aside and sat down in her beautiful dress to feed the lamb. Then look behind her at the short man with the ragged coat, carrying the baby birds.

Look on **through** the archway into a calm and distant scene. A grand house is surrounded by the shining water of a wide moat. A drawbridge crosses the water and people are strolling about on the grass and under the trees. Do you feel that you have suddenly entered another painting?

How would you describe the expressions on the faces of the two men?

Can you spot the artist's signature?

Look how cleverly the artist has created the texture of feathers, tree bark and clothes. Use thick paint, collage or pastels to make your own texture picture.

The Poultry Yard – Jan Steen

Look Behind

At first glance this seems to be a straightforward picture of a hard-working kitchen maid who has thoroughly cleaned and polished her pots, pans, dishes, bowls and jugs.

Is there anything more to find out? What is that man up to as he peeps round the doorway?

Look **behind** the wooden room partition. Can you see a hat wobbling on top of a stick? The man is teasing the kitchen maid, trying to make her look up from her hard work.

The Scullery Maid – **unknown artist**

What do you think will happen next? Is the maid furious at being interrupted, or is she delighted to have her mind taken off her work? Write the story of the picture and give it your own ending.

The Graham Children –
William Hogarth

Four children from the same family pose for this portrait. Robert is playing an instrument called a 'bird organ' to amuse (or confuse!) the caged goldfinch, while Henrietta dances to the music. Anna Maria is tempting the baby Thomas by holding cherries just out of his reach.

But look – what is happening **behind** them? The cat has clawed its way up the chair; its gleaming eyes gaze menacingly at the bird as it prepares to pounce. This little background drama gives a slightly threatening feel to an otherwise homely picture.

The Graham children had a comfortable home, but do you think they would have been able to play in the same way that you do? How would their lives have been different?

Look Close Up

Queen Victoria asked the most famous animal painter of the time to make a portrait of her handsome dog, Eos.

The artist certainly knew how to look **close up**, because he had learned his great skill in drawing animals by actually dissecting them to understand how the muscles and bones form their shape. The artist has given this sleek, alert animal a personality all of its own; it is an individual and not just any dog.

Look at the contrast between the dog's soft, delicate feet and the hard, shiny floor; and the contrast between the limp glove fingers on the stool and the stiff little stool feet. Do you think that the slim, elegant head of Eos might easily slip through the beautiful collar?

Which animal might the wooden stool feet belong to?

Look close up. Can you see the shape of the dog's ribs underneath the gleaming, velvety-black hair?

How would you describe the dog's pose and expression?

18

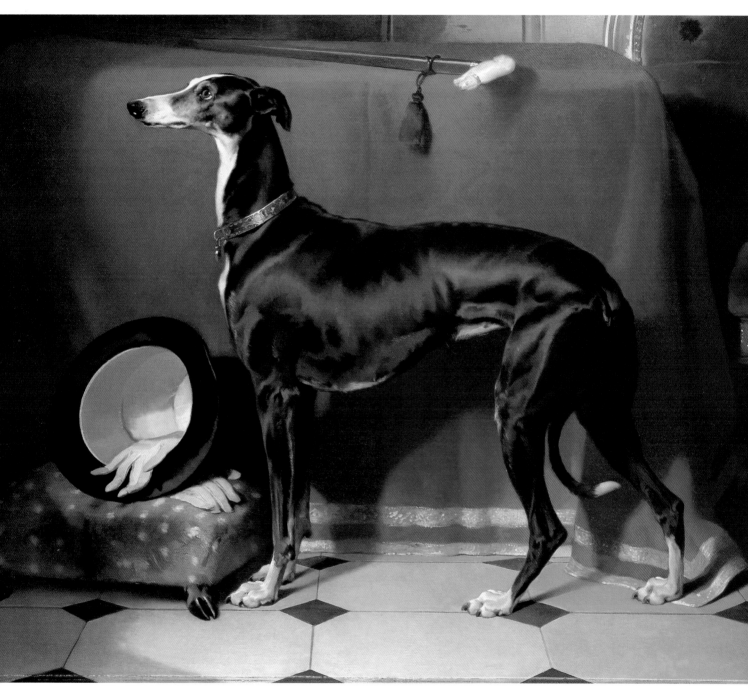

Eos – **Sir Edwin Landseer**

Hunters in the Snow – Pieter Bruegel, the Elder

Look All Around

Three hunters trudge wearily homewards at the end of the day. You can almost hear their snow-crunching footsteps as they plod down the steep hill in the icy stillness.

They pass an inn where a pig is being roasted over a blazing fire. Imagine how the tired hunters and their hungry dogs feel about the delicious smells and comforting warmth.

Look **all around** this winter landscape. It stretches across distant flat lands as far as the eye can see, to craggy mountain peaks. It is full of interesting details for you to discover.

Look very carefully. Can you find:

★ a horse-drawn wagon trundling along a tree-lined road?
★ four churches in the distance?
★ a bridge crossing the winding river?
★ an old woman with a heavy load of twigs on her back?
★ icicles on one of the steep roofs?

Look at how the river has flooded some fields. The water has frozen hard into ice lakes. Despite the freezing temperatures, the villagers are enjoying themselves playing games and skating.

Do you think the woman in a red skirt, being pulled over the ice on a sledge, is having fun?

Look Quickly

You can see straight away how the artist has tried to show movement at great speed. The little dog's legs are frantically trying to keep up with his striding owner. You may think that the artist has chosen a very odd view to paint. He is trying to solve the extremely tricky problem of how to show 'movement' in a painting.

Look at the way the dog's lead makes a delicate swirling pattern as it whisks backwards and forwards, adding to the general feeling of rushing along at a fast pace.

At the time this picture was painted all sorts of fast new machines, such as racing cars, were being invented. This artist was fascinated by speed.

Each one of the dog's tails shows a different position as it frantically bobs up and down. How many tails can you count?

Do a small drawing on the very edge of every sheet of paper in a pad, making each one slightly different. When you quickly flick through the pad you will get the impression of a moving image.

The moving picture that you see at the cinema is actually a series of still images shown very rapidly, one after the other. This is why cinema used to be nick-named 'the flicks'.

Dynamism of a Dog on a Lead – **Giacomo Balla**

Look Again

This is a perfectly straightforward painting of vegetables… or is it? Look **again**, and you may find there's more to it than meets the eye.

Keep looking until you find a gardener with a grinning mushroom mouth. Clue: a bowl makes a good hat!

Does the gardener seem ugly, or curiously strange and interesting to you?

Try drawing an upside-down picture. Start with an oval for a man's head. Put hair at the top and a beard at the bottom. Then draw forehead lines opposite the mouth. By cleverly arranging the nose and eyes you can make a face either way up.

The Vegetable Gardener – **Giuseppe Arcimboldo**

Winter – **Giuseppe Arcimboldo**

Winter is at the end of the year just as old age is at the end of life, so the artist has blended the two ideas into one painting. Everything in this picture looks almost real enough to touch. This sort of skill is called *trompe-l'oeil* (pronounced 'tromp luy'), a French expression that means 'to deceive the eye'.

Try to make a portrait that matches your own favourite season.

Look and **Stare**

As you **stare** at this portrait, the eyes of Vincent van Gogh stare straight back at you.

Van Gogh was very poor. He couldn't afford to pay for an artist's model and so he painted himself. In two years he made twenty-two self portraits!

Just look at these brush strokes. They seem to be wildly flying about in all directions. Do you get the feeling that Van Gogh painted in a fast and furious way? Look closer and notice the way curved brush strokes create the rounded hat shape, while thin diagonal strokes streak across the cheek and fat stubby strokes make the bristly beard. The background could have been plain and ordinary, but even this space is made full of movement by excited paint strokes.

Try this: Lightly sketch a face, then mix some gorgeous, clear paint colours. Use a thin brush for the features to help you control the paint, and broader brushes for the rest. Don't be afraid to use narrow strips of bright colour right next to each other. Keep your eye on this picture of Vincent van Gogh all the time, to give you an idea of how to mould the face with your brush strokes.

You needn't worry about being too exact – just concentrate on making a lively impression.

Self Portrait – **Van Gogh**

Rachel and Jacob at the Well – **unknown artist**

Look, but **Peep**

There is a feeling in this picture that the artist has let us look into a private and special moment in the lives of two young people who are falling in love.

In the Bible story, Jacob met Rachel as she came to water her father's sheep at the well. He helped her by moving the stone away from the mouth of the well and giving the sheep water. Then "he kissed her and was moved to tears," and wanted to marry her.

Rachel's father was reluctant to part with his daughter and made Jacob agree to work as his herdsman for seven years before he and Rachel could marry. Even then, Jacob was tricked at the wedding into marrying Rachel's older sister, Leah, whom he did not love. Jacob had to work for her father for yet another seven years before he could finally marry Rachel.

Look at the way the artist has slightly blurred all the shapes. There are no hard edges or sharp outlines. Colours gently blend together. The picture has an overall softness about it which exactly suits the tenderness of the kneeling couple.

Artists often try to capture an intimate moment. It might be when someone is washing, or dressing, or ill, or sad, or praying. Sometimes it is a happy moment, perhaps when a mother holds her new baby, or a child plays with a pet. What sort of private moment would you choose to draw?

Can you see the way the figures make a triangle shape in the centre, with curving trees on each side? This design gives the picture balance and symmetry.

Look If You Can

Look at this picture if you can. Does it make your head spin? How long can you concentrate on it before looking away?

As you gaze at the wavy lines, the picture begins to swim before your eyes, and this is exactly the powerful effect the artist intends. Bridget Riley is interested in the way certain arrangements of lines, shapes and colours affect our eyes. Her huge pictures seem to move with a regular, pulsating beat.

Look at the picture from a distance; then look at it from above; then tip it at an angle and look again. Each time it makes a different pattern.

Cataract, the name of this piece, means a gushing waterfall or a massive downpour of rain. Do you think the picture is well named? Bridget Riley's paintings are more than scientific experiments about the way our eyes see things: they also remind us of nature.

Imagine how long it must take to paint something as symmetrical and as perfect as this! The work is so slow that the artist often uses assistants to help turn her complicated designs into enormous paintings.

Can you think of another good name for this picture?

Try an eye-dazzling picture by experimenting with close-drawn lines in black pen. To get started, cover all but one corner of this painting over. On your paper, copy the pattern of the tiny portion remaining. You will soon see how to make endless variations of your own.

Cataract 3 – **Bridget Riley**

Look Inwards

When Kandinsky painted this, he was not looking at anything around him to give him ideas. Nor was he painting from memory. He was definitely not suggesting that the shapes in his picture had any sort of secret meaning. You don't need to know a special code to work out what each shape stands for.

Yet Kandinsky was, in a way, looking at something. Perhaps you have already guessed it. He was looking **inwards** at his own mind – at his own imagination. He deliberately set out to paint the shapes and colours that were in his thoughts.

We are used to art like this and so it is hard to believe that in his time, Kandinsky's paintings upset many people. He was the first artist to show that a painting could be about colour and shape alone.

He loved colour, and could remember the colours of the toys he played with when he was three years old: "Light juicy green, white, crimson red and yellow ochre," but not what the toys were. He vividly remembers the intense pleasure of first seeing the bright, fresh colour of paint being squeezed out of a tube.

Have you ever closed your eyes when listening to music and let wonderful designs come into your mind? As you fall asleep, have you ever seen marvellous patterns in your head? When you doodle absent-mindedly with a pencil on a scrap of paper, are you surprised at the amazing designs you make?

You only need to look as far as your imagination for fantastic art ideas. Try it!

Sept – **Vassily Kandinsky**

Look It Up

Here you can find out more about the art and artists in this book, including when the paintings were made, when the artists lived, and where you can see the paintings.

Page 6
The Flying Codonas, 1932
JOHN STEUART CURRY (1897–1946)
Whitney Museum of American Art, New York

An American artist from the mid-west, Curry first trained as an illustrator and was particularly keen on scenes celebrating life in small-town America, far away from the big city. Later he became greatly influenced by the paintings of Rubens, and this led him to develop a swirling, energetic and dramatic style of painting.

Page 7
Windows, 1951
CHARLES SHEELER (1883–1965)
Private Collection, San Francisco, California

Finding it hard to make a living as an artist, Sheeler, an American, became a photographer. His photographs soon began to influence the way he painted, which became precise and exact, using unusual viewpoints. His pictures do not include people, yet even their still emptiness gives us a strong feeling of city life.

Page 8
Three Clowns in a Ring, 1944
GEORGES SCHREIBER (1904–1977)
The Metropolitan Museum of Art, New York
(George A. Hearn Fund, 1945. 45.34.6)

Schreiber was born in Brussels, Belgium. He
studied all over Europe, then moved to New York
at the age of 24. He went on to win prizes for his
work, all over America. As well as being a painter,
he was a lithographer, teacher and an author and
illustrator of several books, including *Bambino the
Clown* which he wrote for his daughter, Joan.

Page 9
Broadway Boogie Woogie, 1942–3
PIET MONDRIAN (1872–1944)
The Museum of Modern Art, New York
(given anonymously)

After experimenting with different styles of painting,
Mondrian gave himself the challenge of painting
only squares, rectangles and perfect straight lines.
He was even more strict with himself about colour,
deciding to use only red, yellow, blue (the primary
colours) with black, white and grey. His style of
painting is instantly recognisable.

Pages 10-11
Train Landscape, 1940
ERIC RAVILIOUS (1903–1942)
Aberdeen Art Gallery and Museum

Ravilious used his artistic talents to be creative in
many different ways. He illustrated books, and
designed furniture, glassware, textiles and even
china for a famous factory called Wedgwood.
Nearly all his pictures are painted in watercolour;
for him oil paint was too thick – he thought it
was like toothpaste! He began with white paper
and painted layers of thin colour until the tones
were deep enough.

Pages 12-13
One of the Family, 1880
FREDERICK GEORGE COTMAN (1850–1920)
Walker Art Gallery, Liverpool

When he was 17, George Cotman exhibited a painting for the first time and it won a prize medal and £5, in those days a large sum of money. After winning five more medals while an art student, he went on to become a popular and successful artist. He painted portraits, landscapes and pictures of ordinary people at home. *One of the Family* is his most famous painting.

Pages 14-15
The Poultry Yard, 1660
JAN STEEN (1625/6–1679)
Mauritshuis, The Hague

Rather than paint religious scenes or grand pictures for grand houses, many Dutch artists preferred to paint scenes of ordinary people doing what they usually do in their everyday life. Weddings, fairs, chicken yards, fish stalls, pastry cooks and milkmaids were Jan Steen's world. Out of his 700 pictures, only a few are landscapes and portraits. Most are set in the home, showing how families lived, or are of people enjoying themselves in taverns.

Page 16
The Scullery Maid,
c. mid 1600s
UNKNOWN DUTCH ARTIST
Dulwich Picture Gallery, London

Page 17
The Graham Children, 1742
WILLIAM HOGARTH (1697–1764)
The National Gallery, London

Hogarth was a superb painter of portraits, but also of other types of picture, especially those that have a strong message, showing us what is right and what is wrong about the way people behave. He thought of each painting as a stage in the theatre, with the people in it acting out a play. Hogarth helped to set up the Foundling Hospital for orphans in London, at a time when unwanted babies were often abandoned.

Pages 18-19
Eos, 1841
Sir Edwin Landseer (1803–1873)
The Royal Collection, Balmoral

Even as a child, Landseer was a brilliant artist and exhibited his first painting at The Royal Academy in London when only 12 years old. His special skill of giving animals almost human expressions made him extremely popular. He was also responsible for the group of huge bronze lion statues at the foot of Nelson's Column in London's Trafalgar Square.

Pages 2-3, 20-21 and Front Cover
Hunters in the Snow, 1565
Pieter Bruegel the Elder
(born c.1523/30; died 1569)
Kunsthistorisches Museum, Vienna

One of the greatest landscape painters, Bruegel's series of five pictures about the seasons is famous. He also liked to paint scenes showing the everyday life of ordinary country people. Many of his pictures are crowded with lively characters, all painted in extraordinary detail. Sometimes he painted in a disapproving way, about drunkenness and greed.

Pages 22-23 **Dynamism of a Dog on a Lead**, 1912
Giacomo Balla (1871–1958)
Albright Knox Art Gallery, Buffalo, New York

An Italian from the city of Turin, Balla did not have an art teacher – he taught himself to paint. He moved to Paris to be with many other artists who were experimenting with new, previously unheard of ways of painting. Balla was searching for an art style for the future, and tried to work out how best to paint speed and movement.

Page 24
The Vegetable Gardener, 1590
GIUSEPPE ARCIMBOLDO (1527–1593)
Museo Civic Ala Ponzone, Cremona, Italy

It is hard to believe that Arcimboldo was making his fantastic dream world paintings nearly five hundred years ago. An artist from the city of Milan in Italy, he painted religious pictures, and designed stained glass and tapestries for the walls of grand rooms. He is best known for his extraordinary heads made up of vegetables, flowers, twigs and leaves.

Page 25
Winter, 1573
GIUSEPPE ARCIMBOLDO (1527–1593)
The Louvre, Paris

Pages 26-27
Self Portrait, 1887
VINCENT VAN GOGH (1853–1890)
The Detroit Institute of Arts

For much of his short life, Van Gogh was poor, depressed and ill. Yet despite this he has left the world hundreds of marvellous drawings and paintings, all made in the last ten years of his life. He worked very fast, his excited brush strokes showing his energy and strong passions. Sadly his work was not liked in his lifetime, and he never knew that he would become one of the most famous artists of all time.

Pages 1, 28-29 and Back Cover (detail)
Rachel and Jacob at the Well, c. mid 1600s
UNKNOWN ARTIST
Dulwich Picture Gallery, London

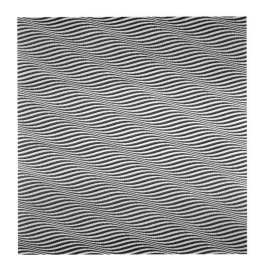

Pages 30-31 **Cataract 3**, 1967
BRIDGET RILEY
(born 1931)
British Council, London

All Bridget Riley's pictures dazzle and disturb your eye with their patterns of spots or wavy lines. Her paintings used to be entirely in black and white and were called 'Op Art'. This is short for 'optical', which means 'to do with sight'. She now uses colour in her enormous pictures of close-packed, swirling lines that seem almost to move as you look at them.

Pages 32-33
Sept, 1943
VASSILY KANDINSKY (1866–1944)
Private Collection

Kandinsky was a Russian-born artist who gave up a career in law to study painting. He was always involved in new ideas about art. He painted the first ever completely abstract pictures, changing our understanding of art forever. He didn't paint the world around him, or anything recognisable; instead, his pictures are about colour and shape alone. These days, this idea is not strange to us. In Kandinsky's time it was astonishing.

Index of Paintings and Artists

Arcimboldo, Giuseppe 24-25

Balla, Giacomo 22-23

Broadway Boogie Woogie 9

Bruegel, Pieter the Elder 20-21

Cataract 3 30-31

Cotman, Frederick George 12-13

Curry, John Steuart 6

Dynamism of a Dog on a Lead 22-23

Eos 18-19

Flying Codonas, The 6

Gogh, Vincent van 26-27

Graham Children, The 17

Hogarth, William 17

Hunters in the Snow 20-21

Kandinsky, Vassily 32-33

Landseer, Sir Edwin 18-19

Mondrian, Piet 9

One of the Family 12-13

Poultry Yard, The 14-15

Rachel and Jacob at the Well 28-29

Ravilious, Eric 10-11

Riley, Bridget 30-31

Schreiber, Georges 8

Scullery Maid, The 16

Self Portrait 26-27

Sept 32-33

Sheeler, Charles 7

Steen, Jan 14-15

Three Clowns in a Ring 8

Train Landscape 10-11

Vegetable Gardener, The 24

Windows 7

Winter 25